Cello Time Sprinters

Cello accompaniment (

Kathy and David Blackwell

Teacher's note

These duet parts are written to accompany the tunes in *Cello Time Sprinters*. They are an alternative to the piano accompaniments or CD, and are not designed to be used with those items.

We are grateful to Alison Ingram and Claire Saddler for all their help in road-testing these duets.

Kathy and David Blackwell

MUSIC DEPARTMENT

OXFORD
UNIVERSITY PRESS

OXFORD
UNIVERSITY PRESS

Great Clarendon Street, Oxford OX2 6DP,
United Kingdom

Oxford University Press is a department of the University of Oxford.
It furthers the University's objective of excellence in research, scholarship,
and education by publishing worldwide. Oxford is a registered trade mark of
Oxford University Press in the UK and in certain other countries

ISBN 978-0-19-340116-7

Cover illustration by Martin Remphry

Music and text origination by Julia Bovee
Printed in Great Britain on acid-free paper by
Halstan & Co. Ltd, Amersham, Bucks.

Contents

1. Carnival jig

KB & DB

2. Spic and span

KB & DB

Variation: try playing with 2 semiquavers to each note:

3. Out of the question

Play questions and answers in this duet, returning to the chorus after each verse.
Make up and write down a question and answer of your own in the 3rd verse. Add your own dynamics!

4. Stop—start

KB & DB

5. River song

KB & DB

Flowing

6. Overture

A Baroque celebration

KB & DB

Allegro

7. Going fourth

KB & DB

8. City streets

KB & DB

9. Minuet

Allegretto

W. A. Mozart (1756–91)

10. Metro line

KB & DB

11. Falling leaves

KB & DB

12. Holiday in Havana

KB & DB

13. Swing low, sweet chariot: next page

14. Night shift

Warily

KB & DB

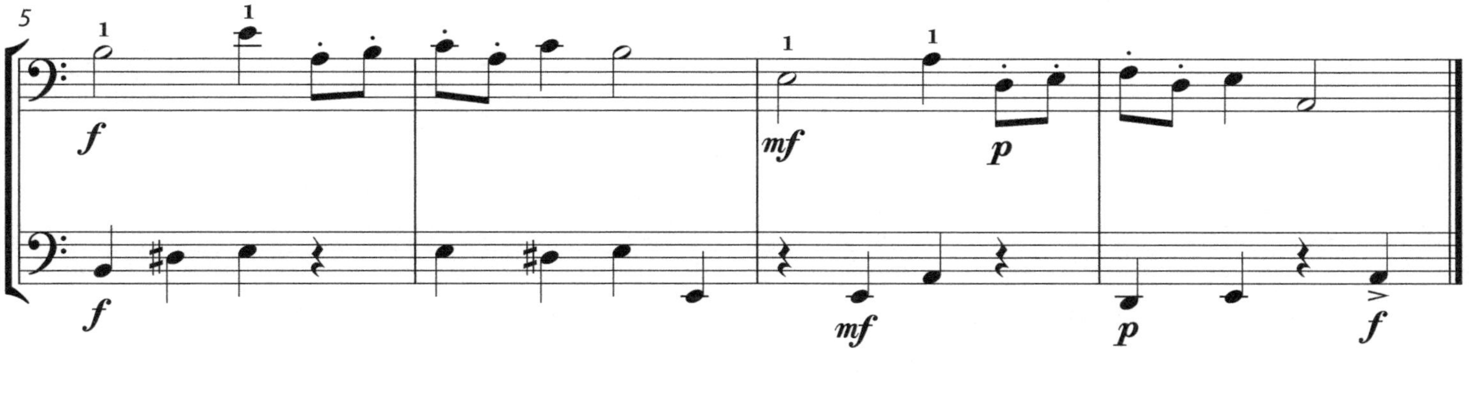

13. Swing low, sweet chariot

Play the second chorus as a canon, with the second part entering after a minim at *.
Count carefully in bar 20! Also try as a canon in 3 or 4 parts.

15. Le Tambourin

J. Ph. Rameau (1683–1764)
(adapted)

16. Scarborough Fair

Wistful

English trad.

17. Beyond the horizon

KB & DB

18. Sto me

Bulgarian trad.

19. Bourrée

G. H. Stölzel (1690–1749)

Adapted from the Clavierbüchlein for Wilhelm Friedemann Bach.

20. Andante

Edward Elgar (1857–1934)

24

21. Joker in the pack

Con brio

KB & DB

22. Sarabande

G. F. Handel (1685–1759)
(adapted)

23. Comin' home

KB & DB

24. Sprint finish

KB & DB

25. In memory

(for Eileen)

KB & DB

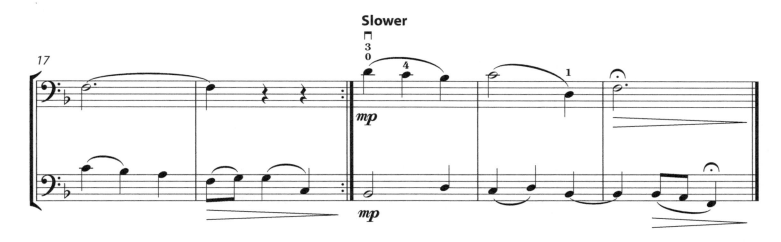

26. Some day

KB & DB

Flowing

27. Wild West

KB & DB

28. Je pense à toi

(*for Clare*)

KB & DB

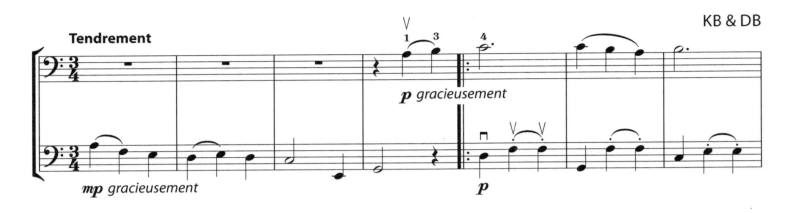

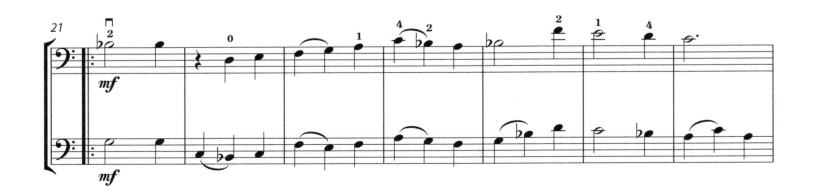

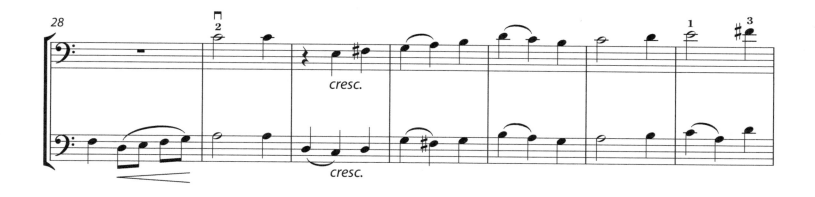

retenu   **très retenu**   **1er mouv^t**

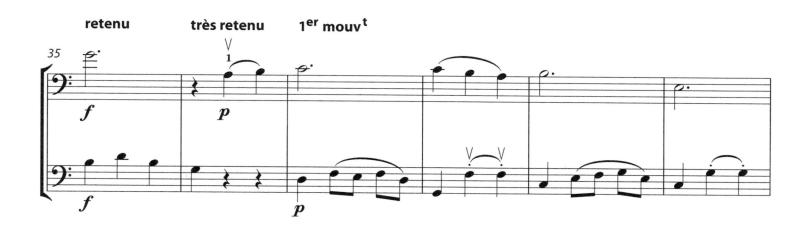

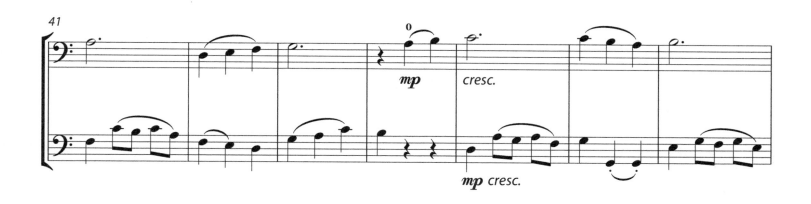

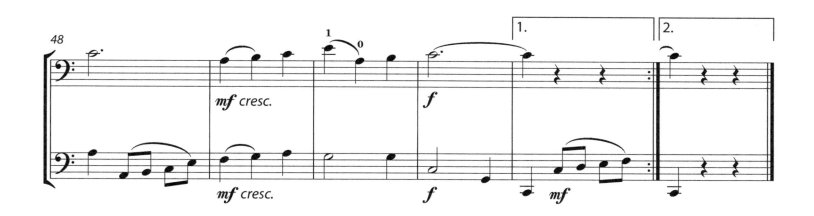

29. Russian wedding

30. Two Songs from Dichterliebe

Robert Schumann (1810–56)
(adapted)

1. The lovely month of May

The repeat is written out in the cello part.

2. The rose and the lily

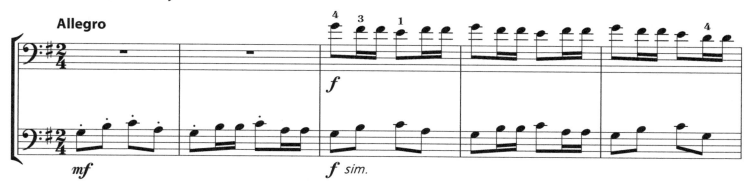

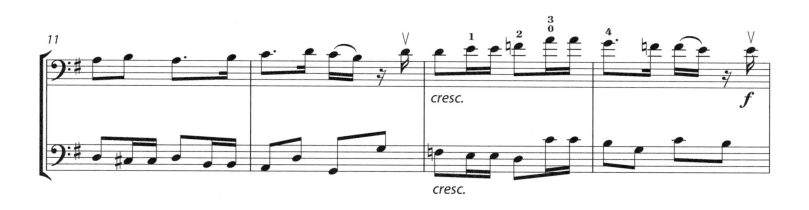

31. Latin nights

Tango

KB & DB

Con fuoco

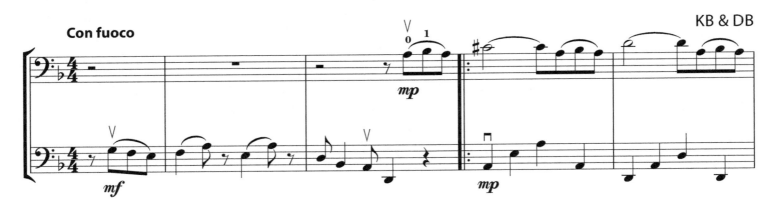

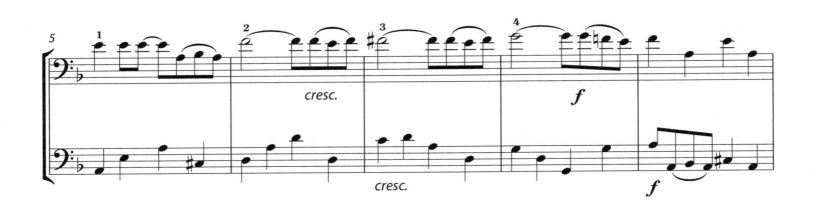

33. Fifth Avenue

(*for Iain*)

KB & DB

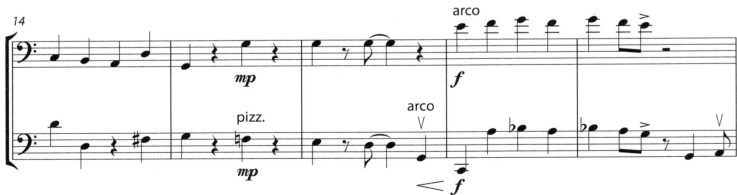

Nos. 32 and 33 are reversed to avoid a page turn.

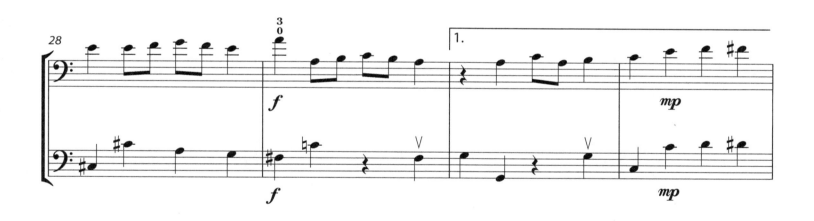

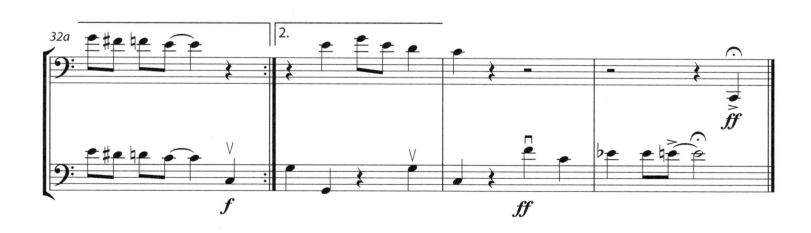

32. 4th dimension

KB & DB

34. Seventh heaven

Dominant seventh study

KB & DB

♩ Tap your cello with your left hand.

35. Jubilate Deo

Play this round in 2 or more parts, entering at *:

W. A. Mozart (1756–91)

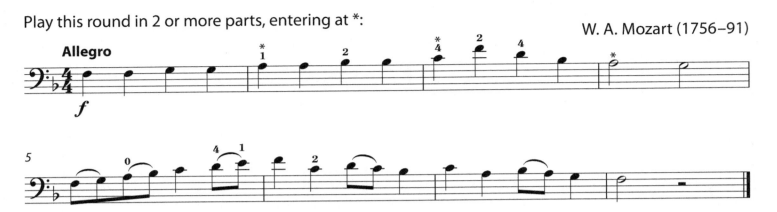

36. Banuwa

Play this round in 2 or more parts, entering at *:

African